THE

WHOOPIE PIE

BOOK

THE
WHOOPIE PIE
BOOK

CLAIRE PTAK

SQUARE PEG

Published by Square Peg 2010

2 4 6 8 10 9 7 5 3

Copyright © Claire Ptak 2010
Photography by Colin Campbell 2010

Claire Ptak has asserted her right under the Copyright, Designs and Patents Act 1988
to be identified as the author of this work

First published in Great Britain in 2010 by
Square Peg
Random House, 20 Vauxhall Bridge Road,
London SW1V 2SA

www.rbooks.co.uk

Addresses for companies within The Random House Group Limited can be found at:
www.randomhouse.co.uk/offices.htm

The Random House Group Limited Reg. No. 954009

A CIP catalogue record for this book is available from the British Library

ISBN 9780224086790

The Random House Group Limited supports The Forest Stewardship Council (FSC), the
leading international forest certification organisation. All our titles that are printed on
Greenpeace approved FSC certified paper carry the FSC logo. Our paper procurement
policy can be found at www.rbooks.co.uk/environment.

Design: Friederike Huber
Photography: Colin Campbell
Food Styling: Claire Ptak
Styling Assistant: Adriana Nascimento

Printed and bound in Italy by Graphicom

For my mom Elisabeth

CONTENTS

INTRODUCTION

A whoopie is not a cookie or a typical cake, and it's definitely not a pie. In fact, no one seems to know WHY it's called a pie. A whoopie pie is somewhere between a cupcake and an ice cream sandwich – a cupcake with the 'icing' in the middle.

Whoopies originated in the US in the 1920s, though their precise birthplace is still under debate. These cake sandwiches have been showing up in the lunch boxes of the Pennsylvania Amish for generations (the story goes that the Amish farmers' wives made them from leftover cake batter as a lunch treat for their husbands) and bakeries and petrol (gas) stations in the state of Maine have been selling them for years. They now have an international following, partly because everyone seems to be in search of a new cake to replace the ever-popular cupcake, but mostly because they are just so delicious.

I love individual cakes that are not too fussy. I make and sell cupcakes, cakes and savoury treats at Violet, my East London bakery. When we added whoopies to the menu, early sceptics were surprised at how soft and moist they were without being overly sweet. This book will show you how to make them at home using fresh, seasonal ingredients, the way I approach all my baking.

The original whoopie combines chocolate cake with a marshmallow filling. American recipes based on this version sometimes use Marshmallow Fluff, a spread which comes in a jar. I've taken that idea and updated it with a completely fresh marshmallow filling made with egg whites, caster sugar and golden syrup, which is then sandwiched between rounds of the softest chocolate cake you've ever eaten.

Typically, whoopies are made in 10cm rounds, just the right size to hold in your hand for eating. I've given instructions for making smaller-sized ones, too – which are perfect for children's tiny fingers, or when you want just a little treat, and great for serving at parties. You'll find plenty of recipes for other whoopie pie bases, too, including pumpkin, strawberry, and mocha, as well as ideas for mouthwatering fillings flavoured with fruit purées or enriched with homemade caramel.

Whoopie pies can also be used to make sticky, gooey puddings, and I've included variations on traditional puds such as rhubarb and custard and banana cream pie. Or the pies can be frozen – my personal favourite – as with my oatmeal ice cream sandwich. The last chapter features a selection of other sweet sandwiches, including peanut butter sandwich cookies and an easy macaroon. I also threw in my favourite brownie recipe, and topped it with ice cream, chocolate sauce and preserved cherries ... why not?

The Amish are given credit for pioneering the idea of putting the icing or frosting inside the cakes to make them easier to transport in lunch boxes. Schoolchildren and farmers are said to have responded to finding these special treats in their lunches with a resounding 'Whoopie!' It's true – these delicious cream-filled treats will make you smile.

SIMPLE & SWEET WHOOPIE PIES

These are all the traditional whoopie pies you may have heard of – plus a few more – that are perfect for a packed lunch or picnic or a tea-time treat. A chocolate whoopie pie filled with marshmallow cream is the quintessential whoopie, although pumpkin and strawberry whoopie pies are now very popular in American bakeries. The kitschy charm of red velvet cake translates well into a whoopie pie, as does carrot cake. The lemon and mocha-orange whoopies are filled with fresh cream and so may not travel as easily, but are as light as air ... and, well, rather addictive.

The whoopie pie that started it all: moist, spongy, dark chocolate cake sandwiched around a fluffy marshmallow centre. Once you taste it, you'll understand what all the fuss is about.

CHOCOLATE WHOOPIE

Filling suggestion: Fluffy Marshmallow (Recipe on page 16)

Makes about 9 large or 24 mini whoopie pies

175g plain flour
100g unsweetened cocoa powder
1½ tsp bicarbonate of soda
½ tsp baking powder
½ tsp salt
125g unsalted butter, softened
200g sugar
1 large egg
225ml buttermilk
1 tsp pure vanilla extract

Preheat the oven to 180°C/gas 4. Line 2 trays with baking paper. In a bowl, sift together the flour, cocoa powder, bicarbonate of soda and baking powder. Stir in the salt and set aside.

In a separate bowl, cream the softened butter and sugar together until light and fluffy, using an electric hand whisk or a freestanding mixer fitted with the flat beater. Add the egg and mix well. Add the buttermilk and vanilla and beat until well combined. Slowly add the dry ingredients in 2 batches, mixing until just incorporated. Chill for 30 mins before using.

Drop 18 large or 48 small scoops of batter, about 5cm apart, onto the prepared baking trays. Bake in the middle of the oven for 10–12 mins for large whoopies or 8–10 mins for mini whoopies, until the cakes are left with a slight impression when touched with a finger.

Remove from the oven to a wire rack and cool completely.

To assemble:
Spread or pipe a generous scoop of Fluffy Marshmallow Filling (page 16) onto the flat surface of a cooled whoopie. Top with another whoopie to make a sandwich, and serve.

FLUFFY MARSHMALLOW FILLING

Makes enough to fill about 9 large or 24 mini whoopie pies

3 egg whites
150g caster sugar
2 tbsp golden syrup
Pinch of salt
1 tsp pure vanilla extract

Weigh all the ingredients into a heatproof bowl (the stainless steel bowl of a freestanding mixer is ideal) and place the bowl over a saucepan of boiling water. Whisk continuously by hand until the sugar has dissolved and the mixture is frothy and slightly opaque (about 10-15 mins).

Remove from the heat and whip the mixture on high speed in a freestanding mixer until it is white and thick and holds its shape.

Use straight away.

This variation combines the richness of cocoa and coffee with the sweet tanginess of candied orange peel for a truly grown-up whoopie pie.

MOCHA-ORANGE WHOOPIE

Filling suggestion: Espresso Cream (Recipe on page 21)

Makes about 9 large or 24 mini whoopie pies

280g plain flour
70g unsweetened cocoa powder
1 tsp bicarbonate of soda
¼ tsp salt
110ml brewed strong coffee
110ml vegetable oil
140ml whole milk
200g caster sugar
1 large egg
175g chopped candied orange peel, plus extra for finishing

Preheat the oven to 180°C/gas 4. Line 2 trays with baking paper.

In a bowl, sift together the flour, cocoa powder and bicarbonate of soda. Stir in the salt and set aside.

In a separate bowl, whisk together the coffee, oil, milk and caster sugar. Whisk in the egg and stir in the candied peel. Slowly add the dry ingredients in 2 batches, mixing until just incorporated. Chill for 30 mins.

Drop 18 large or 48 small scoops of batter, about 5cm apart, onto the prepared baking trays. Bake in the middle of the oven for 10–12 mins for large whoopies or 8–10 mins for mini whoopies, until the cakes are left with a slight impression when touched with a finger.

Remove from the oven to a wire rack and cool completely.

To assemble:
Spread a generous scoop of Espresso Cream (page 21) on the flat surface of a cooled whoopie. Top with another whoopie to make a sandwich. Once filled, chill for 10 mins before rolling the sides of the whoopies in the extra candied peel.

ESPRESSO CREAM

Makes enough to fill about 9 large or 24 mini whoopie pies

340ml double cream
2 tbsp caster sugar
50ml strong brewed coffee, chilled
Scraped seeds of ½ vanilla pod
½ tsp pure vanilla extract
1 tbsp finely ground espresso beans

Combine the double cream and caster sugar in a bowl and whip to very soft peaks, using an electric hand whisk or a freestanding mixer.

Add the coffee, vanilla seeds and vanilla extract and whip again to soft peaks. Fold in the espresso beans and check the consistency. The cream should be thick enough to hold its shape without starting to turn to butter. (If it does get too thick, add a little unwhipped double cream.)

Chill in the fridge for 10 mins before using. The cream will keep for a few days in a sealed container in the fridge, but may need to be rewhipped before using.

Pumpkin is one of our most popular whoopie flavours at Violet. The spicy cake and its tangy cream cheese filling make the perfect pairing, especially in late autumn or early winter.

PUMPKIN WHOOPIE

Filling suggestion: Cream Cheese (Recipe on page 24)

Makes about 9 large or 24 mini whoopie pies

280g plain flour
½ tsp bicarbonate of soda
1 tsp baking powder
1 tsp cinnamon
1 tsp ginger
¼ tsp cloves
¼ tsp mace
¼ tsp ground star anise (if available)
½ tsp salt
200g dark brown sugar
115ml vegetable oil
250g pumpkin purée, fresh or tinned
65ml whole milk
1 egg

Preheat the oven to 180°C/gas 4. Line 2 trays with baking paper.

In a large bowl, whisk together the flour, bicarbonate of soda, baking powder, spices and salt, breaking up any clumps and making sure the raising agents and spices get well mixed in.

In a separate bowl, combine the brown sugar, vegetable oil, pumpkin purée and milk until smooth. Add the egg and whisk to combine. Gradually add the dry ingredients, mixing well until fully incorporated. Chill for 30 mins.

Drop 18 large or 48 small scoops of batter, about 5cm apart, onto the prepared baking trays. Bake in the middle of the oven for 10–12 mins for large whoopies or 8–10 mins for mini whoopies, until the cakes are left with a slight impression when touched with a finger.

Remove from the oven to a wire rack and cool completely.

To assemble:
Spread a generous scoop of Cream Cheese Filling (page 24) on the flat surface of a cooled whoopie. Top with another whoopie to make a sandwich, and serve.

CREAM CHEESE FILLING

Makes enough to fill about 9 large or 24 mini whoopie pies

300g icing sugar
55g unsalted butter, softened
115g cream cheese, softened
½ tsp pure vanilla extract
1 tsp maple syrup (optional)

Sift the icing sugar in a bowl and set aside.

In a separate bowl, whip the softened butter until smooth and creamy with no lumps, using an electric hand whisk or a freestanding mixer fitted with the flat beater. Add the cream cheese and whip together, scraping down the bowl once. Gradually add the sifted icing sugar until the mixture comes together in a light and fluffy texture. Add the vanilla and the maple syrup (if using) and mix well.

Use right away or chill until ready to use. Will keep in a sealed container in the fridge for up to 7 days.

I'm not usually a fan of cooked strawberries, but this is one of my favourite whoopies. A cross between strawberry shortcake and a muffin, it's a great one for the strawberry season.

STRAWBERRY WHOOPIE

Filling suggestion: Strawberry Buttercream (Recipe on page 28)

Makes about 9 large or 24 mini whoopie pies

100g fresh ripe strawberries
300g plain flour
1½ tsp bicarbonate of soda
½ tsp baking powder
¼ tsp salt
200g light brown sugar
75ml vegetable oil
65ml buttermilk
1 egg
Icing sugar for dusting

Preheat the oven to 180°C/gas 4. Line 2 trays with baking paper.
    Put the strawberries in a food processor and pulse until they are chopped but not puréed. Set aside. In a bowl, sift together the flour, bicarbonate of soda and baking powder. Stir in the salt and set aside.
    Combine the brown sugar and oil in a large bowl and mix well with a wooden spoon. Stir in the chopped strawberries and the buttermilk until just combined, then whisk in the egg. Fold in the flour mixture in 2 batches, taking care not to over-mix the batter. Chill for 30 mins.
    Drop 18 large or 48 small scoops of batter, about 5cm apart, onto the prepared baking trays. Bake in the middle of the oven for 10–12 mins for large whoopies or 8–10 mins for mini whoopies, until the cakes are left with a slight impression when touched with a finger.
    Remove from the oven to a wire rack and cool completely.

To assemble:
Spread a generous scoop of Strawberry Buttercream (page 28) on the flat surface of a cooled whoopie. Top with another whoopie to make a sandwich, dust with icing sugar and serve.

STRAWBERRY BUTTERCREAM

Makes enough to fill about 9 large or 24 mini whoopie pies

50ml unstrained strawberry purée (about 80g unhulled berries)
90g very soft butter
500–750g icing sugar, sifted
½ tsp pure vanilla extract
½ tsp lemon juice

Rinse and hull the strawberries, then purée them in a food processor.
    In a bowl, cream together the butter and 300g icing sugar with an
electric hand whisk or on a low speed in a freestanding mixer fitted
with the flat beater. Gradually add the vanilla, lemon juice and strawberry purée. Gradually mix in another 200g icing sugar on a low speed
for about 3 mins, until the mixture has a light and fluffy texture and
the sugar has dissolved. Add more sugar if the mixture seems too soft
(the amount needed varies according to the air temperature and
acidity of the fruit).
    Use right away or store in a sealed container in the fridge for up to 7
days. Bring it to room temperature before using and beat on a low speed
to make it creamy again.

When these are freshly baked and the weather is warm, the melt-in-your-mouth softness of the chocolate chips is simply sensational.

CHOCOLATE CHIP WHOOPIE

Filling suggestion: Chocolate Marshmallow (Recipe on page 32)

Makes about 9 large or 24 mini whoopie pies

280g plain flour
1 tsp baking powder
1½ tsp bicarbonate of soda
¼ tsp salt
125g unsalted butter, softened
100g caster sugar
100g light brown sugar
1 large egg
120ml buttermilk
1 tsp pure vanilla extract
200g dark chocolate chips

Preheat the oven to 180°C/gas 4. Line 2 trays with baking paper. In a bowl, sift together the flour, baking powder and bicarbonate of soda. Stir in the salt and set aside.

In a separate bowl, cream the softened butter and sugars together until light and fluffy, using an electric hand whisk or a freestanding mixer fitted with the flat beater. Add the egg and mix well. Measure the buttermilk into a jug and add the vanilla. Pour this into the butter mixture and beat until well combined. Slowly add the dry ingredients in 2 batches, mixing until just incorporated. Stir in the chocolate chips. Chill for 30 mins.

Drop 18 large or 48 small scoops of batter, about 5cm apart, onto the prepared baking trays. Bake in the middle of the oven for 10–12 mins for large whoopies or 8–10 mins for mini whoopies, until the cakes are left with a slight impression when touched with a finger.

Remove from the oven to a wire rack and cool completely.

To assemble:
Pipe or spread a generous scoop of Chocolate Marshmallow Filling (page 32) on the flat surface of a cooled whoopie. Top with another whoopie to make a sandwich, and serve.

CHOCOLATE MARSHMALLOW FILLING

Makes enough to fill about 9 large or 24 mini whoopie pies

100g dark chocolate, broken into small pieces
3 egg whites
150g caster sugar
2 tbsp golden syrup
Pinch of salt
1 tsp pure vanilla extract

Melt the chocolate in a heatproof bowl over a pan of barely simmering water. Once the chocolate has melted, take the bowl off the pan and let it cool slightly while you prepare the marshmallow.

Place the saucepan of water back on the heat and bring to a boil. Weigh the remaining ingredients into the stainless steel bowl of a freestanding mixer and then place the bowl over the pan. Whisk continuously by hand until the sugar has dissolved and the mixture is frothy and slightly opaque (about 10–15 mins).

Remove the bowl from the heat and transfer to the mixer. Whip the mixture on high speed until it is white and thick and holds its shape. Fold in the melted chocolate.

Use straight away.

We tend to think of carrot cake as a healthier option than other cakes simply because it has a vegetable in it, and we generally feel less guilty about eating it, too. The same goes for this carrot cake whoopie.

CARROT CAKE WHOOPIE

Filling suggestion: Orange Mascarpone Cream (Recipe on page 36)

Makes about 9 large or 24 small whoopie pies

250g plain flour
1 tsp bicarbonate of soda
½ tsp baking powder
½ tsp cinnamon
½ tsp ground ginger
¼ tsp salt
125g unsalted butter, softened
100g caster sugar
100g light brown sugar
1 large egg
1 tsp pure vanilla extract
2 carrots, peeled and grated
Zest of 1 orange

Preheat the oven to 180°C/gas 4. Line 2 trays with baking paper.
    In a bowl, sift together flour, bicarbonate of soda, baking powder, cinnamon and ginger. Stir in the salt and set aside.
    In a separate bowl, cream the softened butter and sugars until light and fluffy, using an electric hand whisk or a freestanding mixer fitted with the flat beater. Add the egg and vanilla and mix well. Add the grated carrot and orange zest and mix well. Finally, add the dry ingredients, mixing until just incorporated. Chill for 30 mins.
    Drop 18 large or 48 small scoops of batter, about 5cm apart, onto the prepared baking trays. Bake in the middle of the oven for 10–12 mins for large whoopies and 8–10 mins for mini whoopies, until the cakes are left with a slight impression when touched with a finger.
    Remove from the oven to a wire rack and cool completely.

To assemble:
Spread a generous scoop of Orange Mascarpone Cream (page 36) on the flat surface of a cooled whoopie. Top with another whoopie to make a sandwich, and serve.

ORANGE MASCARPONE CREAM

Makes enough to fill about 9 large or 24 mini whoopie pies

250g full-fat cream cheese
150g mascarpone cheese
100g icing sugar
Zest and juice of ½ orange

Place the cream cheese in a bowl and whisk until smooth. Add the mascarpone cheese and whisk again.

Sift the icing sugar into the bowl to make sure there are no lumps, and mix until smooth. Add the orange zest and juice and mix to combine.

Use straight away, or store in a sealed container in the fridge for up to 3 days.

Lemon imparts a lovely fresh flavour to cakes and puddings. It's worth seeking out good-quality lemons. The large knobbly ones grown on the Amalfi coast of Italy are exceptional as are the California Meyer lemons.

LEMON CREAM WHOOPIE

Filling suggestion: Lemon Curd Cream (Recipe on page 40)

Makes about 9 large or 24 mini whoopie pies

300g plain flour
1 tsp baking powder
¼ tsp bicarbonate of soda
¼ tsp salt
125g unsalted butter, softened
200g caster sugar
1 large egg
1 tsp pure vanilla extract
100ml whole milk
50ml lemon juice
Zest of 2 medium lemons

Preheat the oven to 180°C/gas 4. Line 2 trays with baking paper.

In a bowl, sift together the flour, baking powder and bicarbonate of soda. Stir in the salt and set aside.

In a separate bowl, cream the softened butter and the sugar together until light and fluffy, using an electric hand whisk or a freestanding mixer fitted with the flat beater. Add the egg and mix well. In a jug, combine the vanilla, milk and lemon juice. Add this to the butter mixture and mix well. Add the dry ingredients, mixing until just incorporated. Finally, fold in the lemon zest. Chill for 30 mins.

Drop 18 large or 48 small scoops of batter, about 5cm apart, onto the prepared baking trays. Bake in the middle of the oven for 10–12 mins for large whoopies or 8–10 mins for mini whoopies, until the cakes are left with a slight impression when touched with a finger.

Remove from the oven to a wire rack and cool completely.

To assemble:
Spread a generous scoop of Lemon Curd Cream (page 40) on the flat surface of a cooled whoopie. Top with another whoopie to make a sandwich, and serve.

LEMON CURD CREAM

Makes enough to fill about 9 large or 24 mini whoopie pies

100g caster sugar
Pinch of salt
Zest and juice of 2 medium lemons
2 egg yolks
125g cold unsalted butter, cut into cubes
50ml double cream

Put the sugar, salt, lemon zest and juice and egg yolks in a medium-sized, heatproof bowl. Place the bowl over a saucepan of barely simmering water and warm gently, whisking constantly. Add the butter, a few cubes at a time, stirring constantly until all the butter is incorporated and the mixture is smooth and thick. Do not overheat or the eggs will scramble. Strain to remove the zest and any eggy bits. Cover with clingfilm, pressing it down on the surface of the custard. Leave to cool for 20 mins, then chill for 2 hours before using.

The lemon curd will keep in a sealed container in the fridge for up to 3 weeks. When ready to use, whip the double cream and fold into the chilled custard.

Every summer my grandmother made me a 'Red Cake' topped with a fluffy white frosting made with a flour roux. This will forever remind me of her.

RED VELVET WHOOPIE

Filling suggestion: Old-fashioned Buttercream (Recipe on page 44)

Makes about 9 large or 24 mini whoopie pies

280g plain flour
50g cornflour
¼ tsp salt
100g unsalted butter, softened
200g sugar
1 large egg
35g cocoa powder
50ml red food colouring
1½ tsp pure vanilla extract
180ml buttermilk
1½ tsp bicarbonate of soda
1½ tsp white vinegar

Preheat the oven to 180°C/gas 4. Line 2 trays with baking paper.
    Sift the flours together and stir in the salt. Set aside.
    In a bowl, cream the butter and the sugar together until light and fluffy with a flat beater. Add the egg and mix well. In another bowl, use a fork to combine the cocoa powder, food colouring and vanilla into a thick paste. Add to the creamed butter and mix well. Add half the buttermilk and mix well. Add half the sifted flour, beating until just mixed. Add the remaining buttermilk, mixing until well combined, then add the remaining flour.
    In a small bowl, dissolve the bicarbonate of soda in the vinegar and add to the cake mixture, scraping it out with a rubber spatula. Beat for a couple of mins but no longer.
    Drop 18 large or 48 small scoops of batter, about 5cm apart, onto the prepared baking trays. Bake in the middle of the oven for 10–12 mins for large whoopies or 8–10 mins for mini whoopies.
    Remove from the oven to a wire rack and cool completely.

To assemble:
Spread a generous scoop of Old-fashioned Buttercream (page 44) on a cooled whoopie. Top with another whoopie, and serve.

OLD-FASHIONED BUTTERCREAM

115ml whole milk
2 tbsp plain flour
100g caster sugar
¼ tsp salt
55g margarine
55g vegetable shortening, such as Trex
1 tsp vanilla extract

Whisk together the milk and flour in a small saucepan, using an electric hand whisk. Place over a moderate heat until the mixture just begins to thicken. Set aside to cool.

In a bowl, beat together the sugar, salt, margarine and shortening until light and fluffy, using an electric hand whisk or a freestanding mixer. Add the vanilla and beat well. Add the flour mixture and beat for 3 mins.

Chill until ready to use. It will keep in a sealed container in the fridge for up to 5 days. Bring to room temperature and beat again with a flat beater before using.

Salted caramel cupcakes are a particular favourite of our male customers at Violet, so we often call it 'the man's cupcake'. Here's a whoopie for the boys.

SALTY CARAMEL WHOOPIE

Filling suggestion: Caramel Swiss Buttercream (Recipe on page 50)

Makes about 9 large or 24 mini whoopie pies

300g plain flour
2 tsp baking powder
½ tsp salt
125g unsalted butter
120ml whole milk
200g light brown sugar
2 large eggs
1 tsp pure vanilla extract

Preheat the oven to 180°C/gas 4. Line 2 trays with baking paper.
    In a bowl, sift together the flour and baking powder. Stir in the salt and set aside. In a small saucepan, melt the butter with the milk but don't let it boil. Remove from the heat and pour into a small bowl to cool.
    In a separate bowl, beat together the brown sugar, eggs and vanilla until light and fluffy, using an electric hand whisk or a freestanding mixer. Add the dry ingredients, mixing until just incorporated. Pour in the cooled milk mixture and stir until just combined. Chill for 30 mins.
    Drop 18 large or 48 small scoops of batter, about 5cm apart, onto the prepared baking trays. Bake in the middle of the oven for 10–12 mins for large whoopies or 8–10 mins for mini whoopies, until the cakes are left with a slight impression when touched with a finger.
    Remove from the oven to a wire rack and cool completely.

To assemble:
Spread a generous scoop of Caramel Swiss Buttercream (page 50) on the flat surface of a cooled whoopie. Top with another whoopie to make a sandwich, and serve.

CARAMEL SWISS BUTTERCREAM

Makes enough to fill about 9 large or 24 mini whoopie pies

40ml double cream
75g caster sugar, plus 50g
2 tbsp water
175g unsalted butter, softened
¼ tsp salt
2 large egg whites
½ tsp pure vanilla extract

Have a whisk and the cream ready to use near the stove.

Combine the 75g caster sugar and the water in a heavy-bottomed saucepan over a medium heat. Swirl the pan occasionally to help dissolve the sugar, but do not stir. Turn the heat up to high and bring the syrup to a boil. Cook, without stirring, until it becomes very dark caramel in colour. Turn off the heat and pour in the cream, whisking continuously (be careful as it will spatter). Transfer to a heatproof container to cool completely.

In a bowl, beat the butter and salt with an electric whisk until fluffy.

In the stainless steel bowl of a freestanding mixer, combine the 50g caster sugar with the egg whites. Place over a saucepan of barely simmering water and whisk continuously by hand until the sugar has dissolved and the mixture is frothy and slightly opaque (about 10–15 mins).

Transfer the bowl of egg whites to the freestanding mixer and whisk until fluffy and cooled (about another 10 mins). Once the mixture is cool enough, start adding the creamed butter. The mixture will curdle but then come back together. Switch to the flat beater and, mixing on medium speed, pour in the caramel.

If not using right away, store in a sealed container in the fridge for up to 5 days. Bring to room temperature and beat with a flat beater before using again.

ICED & GLAZED WHOOPIE PIES

Whoopie pies are, by design, quite plain looking: – a simple sandwiching of cake and filling. Adding a thin glaze dotted with crushed rose petals or piped melted chocolate transforms them into something really beautiful. I've also slipped in a meringue here and although, technically, it's not a whoopie pie, its size and shape are so similar that I thought it made a nice addition to this chapter. These whoopies, served in individual paper cases and stacked in towers on cake stands, would be great for a wedding or celebration.

Inspired by the classic Tunnock's Teacake, this whoopie comprises soft, rich vanilla cake, fluffy marshmallow filling and chocolate glaze, to create an indulgent, retro-style pie.

TEACAKE WHOOPIE

Filling suggestion: Fluffy Marshmallow (Recipe on page 16)
Glaze suggestion: Chocolate (Recipe on page 56)

Makes about 9 large or 24 mini whoopie pies

280g plain flour
¼ tsp baking powder
¼ tsp bicarbonate of soda
A pinch of salt
150g unsalted butter, softened
125g caster sugar
3 large egg yolks
50ml double cream
1 tsp pure vanilla extract

Preheat the oven to 180°C/gas 4. Line 2 trays with baking paper.

In a bowl, sift together the flour, baking powder and bicarbonate of soda. Stir in the salt and set aside.

In the bowl of a freestanding mixer fitted with the flat beater, cream the softened butter and the sugar until light and fluffy. Add the egg yolks, one at a time, and mix well. Measure the cream into a jug and stir in the vanilla. Pour the liquid into the butter mixture and beat until well combined. Add the dry ingredients in one batch, mixing until just incorporated. Chill for 30 mins.

Drop 18 large or 48 small scoops of batter, about 5cm apart, onto the prepared baking trays. Bake in the middle of the oven for 10–12 mins for large whoopies or 8–10 mins for mini whoopies, until the cakes are left with a slight impression when touched with a finger.

Remove from the oven to a wire rack and cool completely.

To assemble:
Spread or pipe a generous scoop of Fluffy Marshmallow Filling (page 16) on the flat surface of a cooled whoopie. Top with another whoopie, then spoon or pipe a generous amount of Chocolate Glaze (page 56) on top. Let the chocolate set completely before serving (up to 1 hour).

CHOCOLATE GLAZE

Makes enough to cover about 9 large or 24 mini whoopie pies

500g milk or dark chocolate, such as Valrhona

Finely chop the chocolate. Place half of the chopped chocolate in a
heatproof bowl that will fit snugly over one of your saucepans.

Pour water into the saucepan to come about 2cm up the sides, and
heat to barely simmering. Place the bowl of chocolate over the pan, to
melt the chocolate, making sure the bottom of the bowl does not come
into contact with the water. Now turn the heat off, but do not remove
the bowl from the pan, as this would release the steam which is needed
to melt the chocolate. Stir the chocolate occasionally to aid the melting.
Once it's melted, add the remaining chopped chocolate and then remove
the bowl from the saucepan. Place the chocolate in a warm part of the
kitchen, away from any draughts, to finish melting. Wait until the
chocolate has melted fully (this will take about 10 mins) before
spooning or piping over the whoopies

The exotic flavours of delicate rose water, tender pistachios and sweet cherry liqueur might seem strange in a whoopie pie, but the evocation of the taste and texture of soft nougat is lovely here.

ROSE-PISTACHIO WHOOPIE

Filling suggestion: Kirsch Swiss Buttercream (Recipe on page 60)
Glaze suggestion: Rose Water Icing (Recipe on page 62)

Makes about 9 large or 24 mini whoopie pies

300g plain flour
1 tsp bicarbonate of soda
½ tsp salt
125g unsalted butter, softened
200g sugar
1 large egg
½ tsp rose water
200ml buttermilk
100g pistachios, finely chopped or ground, plus extra for sprinkling
100g ground almonds
crushed candied rose petals, for garnishing

Preheat the oven to 180°C/gas 4. Line 2 trays with baking paper.
    In a bowl, sift together the flour and bicarbonate of soda. Stir in the salt and set aside. In a separate bowl, cream together the butter and sugar until light and fluffy, using an electric hand whisk or a freestanding mixer fitted with the flat beater. Add the egg and mix well. Measure the rose water and buttermilk into a jug and then add half of this to the butter mixture. Slowly add the dry ingredients, mixing until just incorporated. Add the remaining buttermilk mixture until well combined and then fold in the ground nuts. Chill for 30 mins.
    Drop 18 large or 48 small scoops of batter, about 5cm apart, onto the prepared baking trays. Bake in the middle of the oven for 10–12 mins for large whoopies or 8–10 mins for mini whoopies, until the cakes are left with a slight impression when touched with a finger.
    Remove from the oven to a wire rack and cool completely.

To assemble:
Pipe or spread a generous scoop of Kirsch Swiss Buttercream (page 60) on the flat surface of a cooled whoopie. Top with another whoopie and drizzle with Rose Water Icing (page 62). Sprinkle with the remaining chopped pistachios and some crushed candied rose petals.

KIRSH SWISS BUTTERCREAM

Makes enough to fill about 9 large or 24 mini whoopie pies

225g unsalted butter, softened
3 large egg whites
100g caster sugar
1 tbsp golden syrup
1 tbsp Kirsh cherry liqueur

In a bowl, beat the butter until fluffy, using an electric hand whisk or a freestanding mixer fitted with the flat beater, and set aside. In the metal bowl of a freestanding mixer, combine the 3 large egg whites with the sugar and golden syrup. Place over a saucepan of barely simmering water and whisk continuously by hand until the sugar has dissolved and the mixture is frothy and slightly opaque (10-15 mins).

Transfer the bowl of egg whites to the freestanding mixer, add the Kirsch and whisk until fluffy and cooled (about 10 mins). Once cool, start adding the creamed butter in batches, whisking well after each addition. The mixture will curdle but then come back together again. Switch to the flat beater and beat for 3 mins more.

Will keep in a sealed container in the fridge for up to 5 days. Bring to room temperature and beat with a flat beater before using.

ROSE WATER ICING

Makes enough to cover about 9 large or 24 mini whoopie pies

200g icing sugar
2 tsp rose water

Sift the icing sugar into a small bowl and then whisk in the rose water until smooth. If you prefer a thicker consistency spread on top of the whoopie, add slightly more icing sugar to adjust.

The Walnut Whip, another nostalgic British treat, is actually a fantastic combination of flavours. This whoopie honours those flavours while improving on the quality of ingredients.

WALNUT WHIP WHOOPIE

Filling suggestion: Vanilla Swiss Buttercream (Recipe on page 66)
Glaze suggestion: Chocolate (Recipe on page 56)

Makes about 9 large or 24 mini whoopie pies

300g plain flour
1 tsp bicarbonate of soda
½ tsp salt
125g unsalted butter, softened
200g sugar
1 large egg
1 tsp pure vanilla extract
200ml buttermilk
100g walnuts, finely chopped or ground, plus extra for garnishing
100g ground almonds

Preheat the oven to 180°C/gas 4. Line 2 trays with baking paper.
    In a bowl, sift together the flour and bicarbonate of soda. Stir in the salt and set aside.
    In a separate bowl, cream together the butter and sugar until light and fluffy, using an electric hand whisk or a freestanding mixer fitted with the flat beater. Add the egg and mix well. Measure the vanilla and buttermilk into a jug and add half of this to the butter mixture. Slowly add the dry ingredients, mixing until just incorporated. Add the remaining buttermilk until well combined, then fold in the ground nuts. Chill for 30 mins.
    Drop 18 large or 48 small scoops of batter, about 5cm apart, onto the prepared trays. Bake in the middle of the oven for 10–12 mins for large whoopies or 8–10 mins for mini whoopies, until the cakes are left with a slight impression when touched with a finger.
    Remove from the oven to a wire rack and cool completely.

To assemble:
Pipe or spread a generous scoop of Vanilla Swiss Buttercream (page 66) on the flat surface of a cooled whoopie. Top with another whoopie, then add a generous piping of Chocolate Glaze (page 56) and garnish with chopped walnuts. Let the chocolate set before serving (up to 1 hour).

VANILLA SWISS BUTTERCREAM

Makes enough to fill about 9 large or 24 mini whoopie pies

225g unsalted butter, softened
3 large egg whites
100g caster sugar
1 tbsp golden syrup
Scraped seeds of ½ vanilla pod
1 tsp pure vanilla extract

In a bowl, beat the butter until fluffy, using an electric hand whisk or a freestanding mixer. In the metal bowl of a freestanding mixer, combine the 3 large egg whites with the caster sugar, golden syrup and the vanilla seeds. Place the bowl over a saucepan of barely simmering water and whisk continuously by hand until the sugar has dissolved and the mixture is frothy and slightly opaque (about 10–15 mins).

Transfer the bowl of egg whites to the freestanding mixer, add the vanilla and whisk until fluffy and cooled (about 10 mins). Once cool, start adding the creamed butter in batches, whisking well after each addition. The mixture will curdle but then come back together again. Switch to the flat beater and beat for 3 mins more.

Will keep in a sealed container in the fridge for up to 5 days. Bring to room temperature and beat with a flat beater before using.

A hot chocolate and an individual Mont Blanc with my mom at Café Angelina in Paris were the inspiration for this whoopie pie. Use a good-quality chestnut spread in the filling or make your own.

MERINGUE WHOOPIE

Filling suggestion: Chestnut Cream (Recipe on page 72)
Icing suggestion: Vanilla Bean Cream (Recipe on page 84)

Makes about 9 large or 24 mini whoopie pies

3 egg whites
¼ tsp salt
½ tsp white vinegar
1 tsp pure vanilla extract
200g caster sugar
1½ tsp cornflour

Preheat the oven to 110°C/gas ¼. Line 2 trays with baking paper.

In the bowl of a freestanding mixer, beat together the egg whites, salt, vinegar and vanilla on a high speed until soft peaks form.

In a separate bowl, whisk the sugar and cornflour together by hand and then add half this mixture to the frothy egg whites. Whisk until very stiff, then add the remaining sugar and cornflour mixture and whisk until smooth and glossy.

Drop 9 large or 24 small scoops of meringue, about 4cm apart, onto the prepared baking trays. Bake in the middle of the oven for about 2½ hours for large whoopies or 1 hour for mini whoopies, until the meringues are baked firm on the outside.

Remove from the oven and immediately transfer the meringues off the baking tray and onto a wire rack, peeling off the baking paper, and leave to cool completely before filling.

To assemble:
Simply break open or use a serrated knife to split each meringue. Spread a generous scoop of Chestnut Cream (page 72) on the bottom half. Top with the other meringue half and then spoon a generous amount of Vanilla Bean Cream (page 84) over the top.

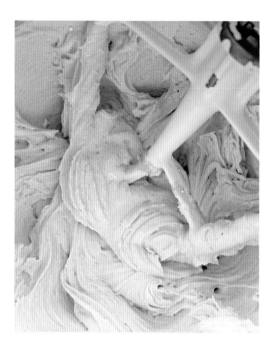

CHESTNUT CREAM

Makes enough to fill about 9 large or 24 mini whoopie pies

100g unsalted butter, softened
100g icing sugar
250g chestnut spread (crème de marrons)
Pinch of salt

Beat together the softened butter and icing sugar until smooth, using an electric hand whisk or a freestanding mixer fitted with the flat beater. Add the chestnut spread and salt and beat until smooth.

The filling can be made ahead and will keep for up to a week in a sealed container in the fridge.

White and frosty, this whoopie pie uses coconut milk and a hit of rum to give it a seriously tropical flavour. Coconut may not be to everyone's taste, but I find the perfume of this gigantic seed intoxicating.

COCONUT CREAM WHOOPIE

Filling suggestion: Coconut Swiss Buttercream (Recipe on page 76)
Icing suggestion: Coconut Glaze (Recipe on page 78)

Makes about 9 large or 24 mini whoopie pies

250g plain flour
2 tsp baking powder
½ tsp bicarbonate of soda
¼ tsp salt
125g unsalted butter, softened
200g sugar
2 large eggs
1 tsp pure vanilla extract
1 tbsp Bacardi white rum
120ml coconut milk
50g desiccated coconut, plus extra for sprinkling

Preheat the oven to 180°C/gas 4. Line 2 trays with baking paper.

In a bowl, sift together the flour and baking powder and bicarbonate of soda. Stir in the salt and set aside.

In a separate bowl, cream the butter and sugar until light and fluffy with an electric hand whisk or in a freestanding mixer fitted with the flat beater. Add the eggs, one at a time, and mix well. In a jug, combine the vanilla, rum and coconut milk. Add this to the butter mixture and mix well. Add the dry ingredients, mixing until just incorporated. Finally, fold in the 50g coconut. Chill for 30 mins.

Drop 18 large or 48 small scoops of batter, about 5cm apart, onto the prepared baking trays. Bake in the middle of the oven for 10–12 mins for large whoopies or 8–10 mins for mini whoopies, until the cakes are left with a slight impression when touched with a finger.

Remove from the oven to a wire rack and cool completely.

To assemble:
Spread a generous scoop of Coconut Swiss Buttercream (page 76) on the flat surface of a cooled whoopie. Top with another whoopie, then spread with Coconut Glaze (page 78) and sprinkle with more coconut.

COCONUT SWISS BUTTERCREAM

Makes enough to fill about 9 large or 24 mini whoopie pies

2 large egg whites
100g caster sugar
¼ tsp salt
1 tbsp golden syrup
175g unsalted butter, softened
40g coconut milk
1 tsp pure vanilla extract
1 tsp Bacardi white rum

Combine the egg whites, caster sugar and salt in the metal bowl of a freestanding mixer. Place over a saucepan of barely simmering water and whisk continuously by hand until the sugar has dissolved and the mixture is frothy and slightly opaque (10–15 mins). Transfer to the mixer and whisk until fluffy peaks form and the mixture has cooled (about 10 mins).

Turn the mixer down to a low speed and add the butter in batches. Mix well after each addition and scrape down the bowl from time to time. The mixture will curdle but then come back together again. Switch to the flat beater and beat for a few mins more. In a jug, whisk together the coconut milk, vanilla and rum. Pour this into the mixture and beat until smooth.

COCONUT GLAZE

Makes enough to cover about 9 large or 24 mini whoopie pies

200g icing sugar, sifted
2 tbsp coconut milk

Sift the icing sugar into a small bowl and then whisk in the coconut milk until smooth. If you prefer a thicker consistency spread on top of the whoopie, add slightly more icing sugar to adjust.

TOPPED & DRIZZLED WHOOPIE PIES

The larger-sized whoopie pie can sometimes be a bit intimidating for one person as a tea-time snack. At Violet we often serve them on a plate with two forks, for a couple or friends to share. This inspired me to create whoopie pies that would make delicious puddings, with billowy cream fillings and drizzled with syrupy sauces. The blackberry-geranium whoopie, which uses fresh, ripe blackberries embellished with rose geranium from the Violet garden, is a particular favourite, while the banana cream pie whoopie is totally decadent.

Flecked with fresh fruit, this stylish whoopie, with its elegant assembly, is a great party pudding for the summer months. Always choose the best fruit available.

RASPBERRY & NECTARINE WHOOPIE

Filling suggestion: Vanilla Bean Cream (Recipe on page 84)
Drizzle suggestion: Raspberry Sauce (Recipe on page 86)

Makes about 9 large or 24 mini whoopie pies

250g plain flour
½ tsp baking powder
1½ tsp bicarbonate of soda
¼ tsp salt
125g unsalted butter, softened
200g sugar
1 large egg
1 tsp pure vanilla extract
50ml whole milk
1 tsp fresh lemon juice
2 small ripe nectarines, stoned and chopped into 5mm dice
100g fresh raspberries, halved
3 small ripe nectarines, cut into wedges, for serving

Preheat the oven to 180°C/gas 4. Line 2 trays with baking paper.

In a bowl, sift together the flour, baking powder and bicarbonate of soda. Stir in the salt and set aside. In a separate bowl, cream the butter and sugar together until light and fluffy, using an electric hand whisk or a freestanding mixer fitted with the flat beater. Add the egg and vanilla and mix well. Measure the milk into a jug and add the lemon juice (the juice will curdle the milk, which is what you want), then beat this into the butter mixture. Gently stir in the prepared fruit. Slowly add the dry ingredients, mixing until just incorporated. Chill for 30 mins.

Drop 18 large or 48 small scoops of batter, about 5cm apart, onto the prepared trays. Bake in the middle of the oven for 10–12 mins for large whoopies or 8–10 mins for mini whoopies, until the cakes are left with a slight impression when touched with a finger.

Remove from the oven to a wire rack and cool completely.

To assemble:
Spread a generous scoop of Vanilla Bean Cream (page 84) on a cooled whoopie. Add the wedges of nectarines and drizzle with Raspberry Sauce (page 86). Top with another whoopie and drizzle with more sauce.

VANILLA BEAN CREAM

Makes enough to fill about 9 large or 24 mini whoopie pies

400ml double cream
2 tbsp caster sugar
Scraped seeds of ½ vanilla pod
1 tsp pure vanilla extract

Put all the ingredients into a large bowl and whisk until the mixture begins to thicken. Taste for sugar and adjust as needed, bearing in mind what other ingredients you will be using to assemble the whoopies and how sweet or 'unsweet' they are.

Chill until needed. Will keep for 3 days in a sealed container in the fridge but may require more whipping before using.

RASPBERRY SAUCE

Makes enough to drizzle over 9 large or 24 mini whoopie pies

300g fresh raspberries
2 tbsp icing sugar
1 tsp kirsch cherry liqueur (optional)

Purée the raspberries and sugar in a food processor or blender, or crush the berries with the back of a wooden spoon, then add the sugar and mix well. Strain the puréed raspberries through a fine mesh sieve and discard the seeds. Stir in the kirsch (if using). Taste and add more sugar if needed.

Chill until ready to use. Will keep in a sealed container in the fridge for 2 days.

Sweet geranium has a delicate flavour that goes well with berries, as in the sauce below, but you may have to grow your own. The leaves are especially fragrant in summer when blackberries are at their peak.

BLACKBERRY WHOOPIE

Filling suggestion: Blackberry Cream (Recipe on page 90)
Drizzle suggestion: Blackberry-Geranium Sauce (Recipe on page 92)

Makes about 9 large or 24 mini whoopie pies

250g plain flour
½ tsp baking powder
1½ tsp bicarbonate of soda
¼ tsp salt
125g unsalted butter, softened
200g sugar
1 large egg
1 tsp pure vanilla extract
50ml whole milk
1 tsp fresh lemon juice
150g fresh blackberries

Preheat the oven to 180°C/gas 4. Line 2 trays with baking paper.

In a bowl, sift together the flour, baking powder and bicarbonate of soda. Stir in the salt and set aside. In a separate bowl, cream the butter and sugar together until light and fluffy, using an electric hand whisk or a freestanding mixer fitted with the flat beater. Add the egg and vanilla and mix well. Measure the milk into a jug and add the lemon juice (this will curdle the milk, which is what you want) and beat this into the butter mixture. Add the dry ingredients, mixing until just incorporated. Chill for 30 mins.

Drop 18 large or 48 small scoops of batter, about 5cm apart, onto the prepared baking trays. Press a few blackberries into each scoop. Bake in the middle of the oven for 10-12 mins for large whoopies or 8-10 mins for mini whoopies, until the cakes are left with a slight impression when touched with a finger.

Remove from the oven to a wire rack and cool completely.

To assemble:
Spread a generous scoop of Blackberry Cream (page 90) on the flat surface of a cooled whoopie. Drizzle with Blackberry-Geranium Sauce (page 92). Top with another whoopie and serve with more sauce.

BLACKBERRY CREAM

Makes enough to fill about 9 large or 24 mini whoopie pies

100g fresh blackberries
2 tbsp caster sugar
½ tsp pure vanilla extract
1 tsp fresh lemon juice
400ml double cream

Put the blackberries, caster sugar, vanilla and lemon juice into a bowl and toss to coat. Use the back of a fork to break up the berries a little. Let the mixture macerate for 10 mins.

Whisk the cream until it just starts to thicken. Fold in the berries and chill for at least 10 mins before using. Use on the same day as making.

BLACKBERRY-GERANIUM SAUCE

Makes enough to drizzle over 9 large or 24 mini whoopie pies

50g caster sugar
50ml water
4 sweet or rose geranium leaves, rinsed and patted dry
400g fresh blackberries

Put the caster sugar and water into a small saucepan and heat to dissolve the sugar, but do not stir. Once the sugar has dissolved, remove the pan from the heat. Drop the geranium leaves into the sugar syrup and steep for about 10 mins.

Purée half the blackberries in a food processor or blender, or crush the berries with the back of a wooden spoon. Add the geranium syrup to the purée and strain the mixture through a fine mesh sieve. Discard the blackberry seeds and geranium leaves.

Add the remaining whole blackberries to the sauce and stir to combine. Chill until ready to use. Best used on the same day as making but will keep in a sealed container in the fridge for up to 2 days.

In this old-time combination of flavours, the rhubarb in the sauce is roasted rather than stewed, which intensifies its tartness, while the sweet vanilla custard filling provides the perfect foil.

RHUBARB & CUSTARD WHOOPIE

Filling suggestion: Vanilla Custard (Recipe for Vanilla Custard Cream on page 106; omit the cream)
Drizzle suggestion: Roasted Rhubarb (Recipe on page 96)

Makes about 9 large or 24 mini whoopie pies

300g plain flour
1½ tsp baking powder
¼ tsp salt
125g unsalted butter, softened
200g sugar
2 large eggs
1 tsp pure vanilla extract
Scraped seeds of ½ vanilla pod
150ml buttermilk
1 tsp bicarbonate of soda

Preheat the oven to 180°C/gas 4. Line 2 trays with baking paper.

In a bowl, sift together the flour and baking powder. Stir in the salt and set aside.

In a separate bowl, cream together the softened butter and sugar until light and fluffy, using an electric hand whisk or a freestanding mixer fitted with the flat beater. Add the eggs, one at a time, and mix well. Mix in the vanilla and the seeds. Measure out the buttermilk in a jug and stir in the bicarbonate of soda. Pour this into the butter mixture and mix well. Add the dry ingredients, mixing until just incorporated. Chill for 30 mins.

Drop 18 large or 48 small scoops of batter, about 5cm apart, onto the prepared baking trays. Bake in the middle of the oven for 10–12 mins for large whoopies or 8–10 mins for mini whoopies, until the cakes are left with a slight impression when touched with a finger.

Remove from the oven to a wire rack and cool completely.

To assemble:
Spread a generous scoop of plain Vanilla Custard (page 106; cream omitted) on the flat surface of a cooled whoopie. Drizzle with Roasted Rhubarb (page 96) and top with another whoopie.

ROASTED RHUBARB

Makes enough to drizzle over 9 large or 24 mini whoopie pies

250g rhubarb
50g caster sugar
1 tsp orange zest
Scraped seeds of ½ vanilla pod

Preheat the oven to 180°C/gas 4.

Cut the rhubarb into 4cm lengths (if they are really fat sticks, slice them through the middle first). Arrange the rhubarb in the bottom of a non-reactive roasting dish and sprinkle with the sugar. Add the orange zest and the vanilla seeds.

Cover the rhubarb with kitchen foil and roast in the oven for 30 mins.

Remove the foil and roast for 20 mins more, to reduce the sauce that will have formed. Leave to cool before using. The rhubarb will keep in a sealed container in the fridge for up to 2 weeks.

Banana cream pie is an American institution. Turning it into a whoopie seems only natural.

BANANA CREAM PIE WHOOPIE

Filling suggestion: Vanilla Custard Cream (Recipe on page 106)
Drizzle suggestion: Chocolate Sauce and Salty Caramel Sauce (Recipes on pages 102 and 104)
Sprinkle suggestion: Chocolate Shavings (Recipe on page 102)

Makes about 9 large or 24 small whoopie pies

280g plain flour
½ tsp baking powder
½ tsp bicarbonate of soda
¼ tsp salt
1 large banana, plus 2 more for serving
150ml crème fraîche
125g unsalted butter, softened
100g sugar
100g light brown sugar
1 large egg

Preheat the oven to 180°C/gas 4. Line 2 trays with baking paper.

In a bowl, sift together the flour, baking powder and bicarbonate of soda. Stir in the salt and set aside. In a separate bowl, mash up one banana, stir in the crème fraîche and set aside.

In another bowl, cream the butter and sugars until light and fluffy with an electric hand whisk or in a freestanding mixer fitted with the flat beater. Add the egg and mix well. Add the banana mixture and beat until combined. Add the dry ingredients until just mixed. Chill for 30 mins.

Drop 18 large or 48 small scoops of batter, about 5cm apart, onto the prepared baking trays. Bake in the middle of the oven for 10–12 mins for large whoopies or 8–10 mins for mini whoopies.

Remove from the oven to a wire rack and cool completely.

To assemble:
Spread a cooled whoopie with Chocolate Sauce (page 102). Add a generous scoop of Vanilla Custard Cream (page 106) and some sliced banana. Drizzle with Salty Caramel Sauce (page 104). Top with another whoopie, more sauce, and sprinkle with Chocolate Shavings (page 102).

CHOCOLATE SAUCE & SHAVINGS

For the sauce
225ml double cream
100g dark chocolate, chopped

For the shavings
100–200g dark chocolate bar (the thicker the bar, the better the
results)

To make the sauce, heat the cream in a small saucepan. Just before it
starts to boil, remove the pan from the heat. Drop the chopped
chocolate into the pan and stir to melt. Let the sauce cool for 15 mins
before using. Once cool, it will keep in a sealed container in the fridge
for up to 5 days.

For the chocolate shavings, leave the chocolate bar in a warmish
place in your kitchen or warm the bar slightly by holding it (still
wrapped) between your hands for a few moments. Use a sharp
vegetable peeler to shave the chocolate bar at a slight angle. You can
shave the chocolate directly onto your whoopies or into a container and
store the shavings in the freezer for up to 3 weeks.

When taking the defrosted shavings from their container, use a spoon
as the warmth of your hands can easily melt the delicate shavings.

SALTY CARAMEL SAUCE

Makes enough to fill about 9 large or 24 mini whoopie pies

2 tbsp cold water
100g caster sugar
120g double cream
25g unsalted butter
Pinch of sea salt

Put the water in a heavy-bottomed saucepan. Add the caster sugar and heat gently to dissolve, swirling the contents around without stirring. Once the sugar has dissolved, turn the heat up to high and bring to the boil. Cook until the caramel is dark, then whisk in the cream, taking care not to splash. Add the butter and salt and whisk until smooth.

Let the sauce cool before using. Will keep in a sealed container in the fridge for 1 week.

VANILLA CUSTARD CREAM

Makes enough to fill about 9 large or 24 mini whoopie pies

Pinch of salt
50g caster sugar
15g cornflour
1 egg
225ml whole milk
½ vanilla pod, seeds scraped
25g unsalted butter, cut into pieces
50ml double cream (omit for a plain vanilla custard)

In a bowl, mix together the salt, sugar and cornflour. Whisk in the egg to
make a paste. In a saucepan, heat the milk, vanilla pod and seeds until
it starts to froth but does not boil. Remove from the heat. Slowly pour
half of the hot milk into the egg mixture, whisking as you go. Now pour
the egg mixture back into the pan of hot milk and whisk. Return to the
heat, whisking until the custard thickens. Strain the custard through a
fine mesh sieve into a heatproof bowl. As it starts to cool, stir in the
butter. Press clingfilm down on the surface of the custard. Leave to cool
for 20 mins, then chill for 2 hours. Will keep for 5 days in a sealed
container in the fridge. Before using, whip the cream and fold into the
chilled custard.

FROZEN & CHILLED WHOOPIE PIES

Ice cream sandwiches are one of the best things in life! The whoopie pie as an ice cream sandwich is a natural evolution. I prefer a soft, cakey ice cream sandwich to a wafery one. These sandwiches can be made using any of the whoopie cake mixes in this book and your favourite ice cream (homemade or shop-bought). I have included two quick and easy ice cream recipes that don't require you to have an ice cream machine, so anyone can make them.

All the flavour of an oatmeal cookie but with a soft whoopie texture, this makes a great treat when sandwiched with vanilla ice cream and frozen, or served at room temperature with strawberry buttercream.

OATMEAL COOKIE WHOOPIE

Filling suggestion: Good-quality vanilla ice cream or Strawberry Buttercream (Recipe on page 28)

Makes 24 bite-sized ice cream whoopie sandwiches

180g plain flour
1 tsp bicarbonate of soda
1 tsp cinnamon
A pinch of salt
225g unsalted butter, softened
200g light brown sugar
2 large eggs
1 tsp pure vanilla extract
200g jumbo oats
75g sultanas (optional)
good-quality vanilla ice cream, for the filling

Preheat the oven to 180°C/gas 4. Line 2 trays with baking paper.
    In a bowl, sift together the flour, bicarbonate of soda and cinnamon. Stir in the salt and set aside.
    In a separate bowl, cream together the butter and light brown sugar until light and fluffy, using an electric hand whisk or a freestanding mixer fitted with the flat beater. Add the eggs, one at a time, and then the vanilla, mixing well. Add the dry ingredients and mix until combined. Add the oats and sultanas and mix until incorporated. Chill for 30 mins
    Drop 48 small scoops of batter, about 5cm apart, onto the prepared trays. Bake in the middle of the oven for 8–10 mins, until the cakes are left with a slight impression when touched with a finger.
    Remove from the oven to a wire rack and cool completely.

To assemble:
Spread a generous scoop of slightly softened vanilla ice cream on the flat surface of a cooled whoopie. Top with another whoopie, gently press together and place in the freezer for at least 15 mins.

The key limes used in the authentic American pie recipe are not easy to find in the UK but you can use any variety of fresh lime juice in this whoopie pie variation.

KEY LIME WHOOPIE

Filling suggestion: Frozen Key Lime Cream (Recipe on page 114)

Makes about 9 large or 24 mini whoopie pies

300g plain flour
1 tsp baking powder
1 tsp bicarbonate of soda
¼ tsp salt
125g unsalted butter, softened
200g caster sugar
1 large egg
100ml whole milk
50ml lime juice
Zest of 2 or 3 limes

Preheat the oven to 180°C/gas 4. Line 2 trays with baking paper.

In a bowl, sift together the flour, baking powder and bicarbonate of soda. Stir in the salt and set aside.

In a separate bowl, cream together the softened butter and the sugar until light and fluffy, using an electric hand whisk or a freestanding mixer fitted with the flat beater. Add the egg and mix well. In a jug, combine the milk and lime juice. Pour half of this liquid into the butter mixture and mix well. Add half of the dry ingredients, mixing until just incorporated, then pour in the remaining milk-lime liquid and mix to combine. Add the rest of the dry ingredients and mix just until incorporated. Finally, fold in the lemon zest. Chill for 30 mins.

Drop 18 large or 48 small scoops of batter, about 5cm apart, onto the prepared baking trays. Bake in the middle of the oven for 10–12 mins for large whoopies or 8–10 mins for mini whoopies, until the cakes are left with a slight impression when touched with a finger.

Remove from the oven to a wire rack and cool completely.

To assemble:
Sandwich together the whoopie cakes with discs of Frozen Key Lime Cream (page 114) and then place in the freezer for at least 15 mins before serving.

FROZEN KEY LIME CREAM

Makes enough to fill about 9 large or 24 mini whoopie pies

6 egg yolks
50g caster sugar
400g sweetened condensed milk
2 tbsp grated lime zest
Freshly squeezed juice of 5 limes

Line the cups of a large or mini muffin tin with clingfilm and place in the freezer.

Beat the egg yolks and sugar on high speed in the bowl of a freestanding mixer fitted with a whisk for 5 mins, until thickened. Now, with the mixer on medium speed, add the condensed milk, lime zest, and lime juice.

Pour or scoop the mixture into the prepared muffin tin and smooth the tops with a palette knife or an offset spatula. Freeze overnight.

This mint chip ice cream sandwich never fails to cheer up friends.
It takes a little preparation but the result is worth it.

CHOCOLATE MINT WHOOPIE

Filling suggestion: Frozen Mint Chip Cream (Recipe on page 118)

Makes about 9 large or 24 mini whoopie pies

175g plain flour
100g unsweetened cocoa powder
1½ tsp bicarbonate of soda
½ tsp baking powder
½ tsp salt
125g unsalted butter, softened
200g sugar
1 large egg
225ml buttermilk
1 tsp peppermint extract

Preheat the oven to 180°C/gas 4. Line 2 trays with baking paper.
     In a bowl, sift together the flour, cocoa powder, bicarbonate of soda
and baking powder. Stir in the salt and set aside.
     In a separate bowl, cream together the softened butter and sugar
until light and fluffy, using an electric hand whisk or a freestanding
mixer fitted with the flat beater. Add the egg and mix well. Add the
buttermilk and peppermint and beat until well combined. Slowly add
the dry ingredients in 2 batches, mixing until just incorporated. Chill
for 30 mins.
     Drop 18 large or 48 small scoops of batter, about 5cm apart, onto the
prepared trays. Bake in the middle of the oven for 10–12 mins for large
whoopies or 8–10 mins for mini whoopies, until the cakes are left with a
slight impression when touched with a finger.
     Remove from the oven to a wire rack and cool completely.

To assemble:
Use a biscuit cutter that's the same size as the cups in your muffin tins
to trim down the whoopies to the same size as the discs of Frozen Mint
Chip Cream (page 118). Sandwich together the whoopies with the
frozen discs and place in the freezer for at least 15 mins.

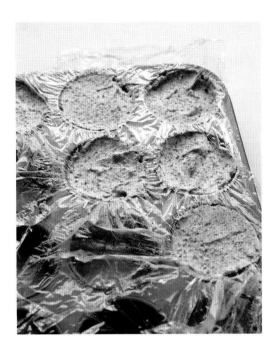

FROZEN MINT CHIP CREAM

Makes enough filling for about about 9 large or 24 mini whoopie pies

200ml double cream
200g sweetened condensed milk
½ tsp peppermint oil
50g dark chocolate

Line the cups of a large or mini muffin tin with clingfilm and place in the freezer.

Beat the double cream to very soft peaks. Whisk in the sweetened condensed milk until smooth. Fold in the peppermint oil, and taste. Add a little more peppermint if you like it slightly stronger. Remember that when the mixture is frozen, the flavours will be more subtle. Use a vegetable peeler or microplane zester to shave thin bits of chocolate into the cream mixture. Fold together and scoop into the prepared tins. Smooth the tops and freeze overnight.

HOLIDAY
WHOOPIE PIES

Christmas cake was a revelation when I moved to London from California, having always thought that fruitcake was sort of a cruel joke. It's now something I look forward to every year and can't get enough of. When made right, it is magnificent. So I just had to make a Christmas cake whoopie pie. Easter and Halloween are my two favourite holidays so they, too, have their own festive whoopies.

These are adorable with a spicy cream in the middle and a pretty glaze on top. Inverted gold paper cases and edible gold balls add an extra festive touch.

CHRISTMAS CAKE WHOOPIE

Filling suggestion: Brown Sugar Spice Buttercream (Recipe on page 124)
Glaze suggestion: Rose Water Icing (Recipe on page 62)

Makes about 9 large or 24 mini whoopie pies

1 tbsp brandy
Zest and juice of ½ orange
50g currants
50g candied peel, chopped
300g plain flour
50g cornflour
1½ tsp bicarbonate of soda
½ tsp mixed spice
¼ tsp cloves
½ tsp salt
125g unsalted butter, softened
200g dark brown sugar
1 large egg
150ml buttermilk
50g ground almonds

Preheat the oven to 180°C/gas 4. Line 2 trays with baking paper.

In a bowl, combine the brandy, orange zest and juice, currants and candied peel. Soak overnight or for at least 2 hours.

In another bowl, sift together the flours, bicarbonate of soda, spices and salt. In a separate bowl, cream the butter and sugar together until light and fluffy. Add the egg and mix well. Add the buttermilk and gently stir in the prepared fruit and ground almonds. Slowly add the dry ingredients, mixing until just incorporated. Chill for 30 mins.

Drop 18 large or 48 small scoops of batter, about 5cm apart, onto the prepared trays. Bake in the middle of the oven for 10–12 mins for large whoopies or 8–10 mins for mini whoopies.

Remove from the oven to a wire rack and cool completely.

To assemble:
Spread a generous scoop of Brown Sugar Spice Buttercream (page 124) on a cooled whoopie. Top with another whoopie and drizzle with Rose Water Icing (page 62). Decorate with a gold ball and gold paper case.

BROWN SUGAR SPICE BUTTERCREAM

Makes enough to fill about 9 large or 24 mini whoopie pies

225g unsalted butter, softened
3 large egg whites
100g dark brown sugar
1 tbsp golden syrup
¼ tsp mixed spice

Beat the butter until fluffy, using an electric hand whisk or a
freestanding mixer fitted with the flat beater. In the metal bowl of a
freestanding mixer, combine the egg whites with the sugar, golden
syrup and mixed spice. Place over a saucepan of barely simmering
water and whisk continuously by hand until the sugar has dissolved
and the mixture is frothy and slightly opaque (10–15 mins).

Transfer the bowl of egg whites to the freestanding mixer and whisk
until fluffy and cooled (about 10 mins). Once cool, start adding the
creamed butter in small batches, whisking well after each addition. The
mixture will curdle but then come back together again. Switch to the
flat beater and beat for 3 mins more. If not using right away, store in a
sealed container in the fridge for up to 5 days. Bring to room
temperature and beat with a flat beater before using.

These are hilarious to make and were inspired by one of my baking icons, Martha Stewart. Get creative – it's scary what you're capable of. You can use any sweets you like to decorate the top.

SPOOKY HALLOWE'EN WHOOPIE

Vanilla Whoopies (Recipe for Easter Egg Whoopies on page 131)
Multi-coloured Buttercreams (Recipe on page 132), using black and
    green food colouring
Liquorice Allsorts
Black liquorice
Coloured and chocolate-covered buttons
Sour tape or belt sweets in red
Mini marshmallows

Bake a combination of large and mini whoopie pies according to the instructions on page 131. For a mix of sizes, use 8 large scoops and 26 small scoops of batter, and bake for 10 mins. This will make 4 large and 13 mini whoopies – but do not assemble them yet.

Now follow the recipe for Multi-coloured Buttercreams on page 132. Separate the buttercream into 3 bowls. Colour one black (which turns out tombstone grey), one green (like slime) and leave the third a ghostly white.

Spread or pipe a generous scoop of one of the coloured buttercream onto the surface of a cooled whoopie. Top with another whoopie. Now use a palette knife to spread the various colours of buttercream on the tops of the pies.

Cut the sweets into shapes with kitchen scissors. Liquorice ropes or round Liquorice Allsorts, thinly snipped, make great eyeballs. Sour tape makes a perfect tongue and mini marshmallows make good teeth.

Stick the sweets however you like into the freshly applied icing so that they stay put.

In the US we have a tradition of hard-boiling white hen's eggs and then dyeing them in pastel colours for Easter Sunday. We hide them in the garden, ready for an Easter egg hunt.

EASTER EGG WHOOPIES

Filling suggestion: Multi-coloured Buttercreams (Recipe on page 132)

Makes 24 mini whoopie pies

280g plain flour
¼ tsp baking powder
¼ tsp bicarbonate of soda
A pinch of salt
150g unsalted butter, softened
125g sugar
1 large egg
1 large egg yolk
100ml whole milk
1 tsp pure vanilla extract

Preheat the oven to 180°C/gas 4. Line 2 trays with baking paper.

In a bowl, sift together the flour, baking powder and bicarbonate of soda. Stir in the salt and set aside.

In a separate bowl, cream the softened butter and sugar together until light and fluffy, using an electric hand whisk or a freestanding mixer fitted with the flat beater. Add the egg and the egg yolk and mix well. Add the milk and vanilla to the butter mixture. Slowly add the dry ingredients, mixing until just incorporated. Chill for 30 mins.

Drop 48 small scoops of batter, about 5cm apart, onto the prepared trays. Bake in the middle of the oven for 8–10 mins, until the cakes are left with a slight impression when touched with a finger.

Remove from the oven to a wire rack and cool completely.

To assemble:
Spread or pipe a generous scoop of one of the Multi-coloured Buttercreams (page 132) onto the flat surface of a cooled whoopie. Top with another whoopie and decorate the sides with rainbow edible balls if desired. Place the assembled whoopies in colourful paper cases in little boxes, baskets, or pretty bowls.

MULTI-COLOURED BUTTERCREAMS

Makes enough to fill 24 mini whoopie pies

225g unsalted butter, softened
3 large egg whites
100g caster sugar
1 tbsp golden syrup
1 tsp pure vanilla extract
Selection of food colourings

In a bowl, beat the butter until fluffy. In the metal bowl of a freestanding
mixer, combine the egg whites with the sugar and golden syrup. Place
over a saucepan of barely simmering water and whisk by hand until the
sugar has dissolved and the mixture is frothy and slightly opaque
(10–15 mins). Transfer the metal bowl to the mixer, add the vanilla and
whisk until fluffy and cooled (about 10 mins). Once cool, start adding
the creamed butter in small batches, whisking well after each addition.
Switch to the flat beater and beat for 3 mins more.

Separate the mixture into 3 or 4 bowls and add different food
colourings of your choice to each bowl. If not using right away, store in
separate sealed containers in the fridge for up to 5 days. Bring to room
temperature and beat with a flat beater before using.

A FEW OTHER SWEET TREATS

Macaroons, brownies, blondies, s'mores and more. These are recipes that I thought you wouldn't want to live without. Not whoopie pies, but delicious treats to make with your children or friends or all by yourself!

These chocolately marshmallow sandwiches get their name from
the pleas of children begging for some-more, or s'more. In the US we
use graham crackers, but digestive biscuits are the next best thing.

S'MORES

Bamboo skewers, or roasting sticks cut from a tree branch
Large marshmallows, from a packet
Your favourite milk or dark chocolate bar, broken into squares
Digestive biscuits

Use bamboo skewers or roasting sticks to toast the marshmallows over
a campfire or gas-burner flame.
    To assemble the s'mores, put a square of chocolate on a digestive
biscuit, place the hot marshmallow on top and cover with another
digestive biscuit, holding down the sandwich and pulling out the
skewer or stick.

This recipe came to me from one of my dearest friends, Lazuli Whitt, courtesy of her mother Barbara. When Lazuli first made this cobbler for us, my husband said it was the best dessert he had ever eaten. Erm . . .

PRIZE PEACH COBBLER

Serves 6

100g plain flour
2 tsp baking powder
Pinch of salt
100g caster sugar, plus an extra 100g
160ml whole milk
100g unsalted butter, melted and cooled slightly
5–6 ripe peaches

Preheat the oven to 190°C/gas 5. Line 2 trays with baking paper.

In a bowl, sift together the flour and baking powder. Stir in the salt and 100g caster sugar and then slowly whisk in the milk. Now whisk in the melted butter in a steady stream to form a pancake-like batter, then set aside.

Bring a saucepan of water to the boil and set up a bowl filled with iced water and a slotted spoon (or spider) next to the stovetop. Once the water in the pan is boiling, gently drop in the peaches (you may need to do this in 2 batches). Blanch the peaches for a minute only and then remove them with a slotted spoon, submerging them in the ice water bath to stop them cooking. Slip off the skins and then quarter and core the peaches and remove the stones. You may want to slice them again if the peaches are large. Pour the extra 100g caster sugar into a bowl, then toss the quartered peaches in the sugar and transfer to a large gratin dish.

Pour the batter over the peaches and bake in the middle of the oven for about 1 hour. The cobbler is ready when it bubbles and turns golden and a skewer inserted comes out clean.

A great idea for a dessert is to bake some brownies, dollop on some vanilla ice cream and top with chocolate sauce, preserved cherries and toasted flaked almonds.

BROWNIE SUNDAE

Makes about 6–12 brownies

300g dark chocolate, chopped
150g unsalted butter
3 eggs
150g dark brown sugar
50g caster sugar
½ tsp sea salt
2 tsp vanilla extract
100g plain flour

For the topping
50g flaked almonds
Good-quality vanilla ice cream
Good-quality cherries in syrup
Chocolate Sauce (Recipe on page 102)

Preheat the oven to 160°C/gas 3. Butter and line a 23cm square cake tin with parchment paper so that it comes up the sides of the tin.

Place the chocolate and butter in a heatproof bowl and melt over a pan of barely simmering water. In another bowl, whisk the eggs, sugars, salt and vanilla until frothy, then whisk in the melted chocolate. Fold in the flour until just mixed, then pour the batter into your prepared baking tin.

Bake in the middle of the oven for about 25 mins. These brownies are better when slightly underdone. A skewer inserted should come out a little wet. Leave to cool completely in the baking tin, then cut into generous-sized squares.

For the topping, toast the flaked almonds lightly in the oven (these will keep for up to a week in a sealed container).

To serve, place a brownie in each serving bowl, add a scoop of vanilla ice cream, then drizzle with chocolate sauce and top with a few cherries. Finish with a sprinkling of toasted flaked almonds.

Blondies have the texture and richness of brownies, but without the chocolate – hence the name. I have snuck in some chunks of milk chocolate here, but the body of the blondie tastes like treacle.

BUTTERSCOTCH BLONDIES

Makes about 16 blondies

350g unsalted butter, softened
320g plain flour
1½ tsp baking powder
1½ tsp sea salt
3 eggs
400g dark brown sugar
2 tsp pure vanilla extract
200g butterscotch milk chocolate bar, chopped into small pieces

Preheat the oven to 160°C/gas 3. Butter and line a 23cm square cake tin with parchment paper so that it comes up the sides of the tin.

Gently melt the butter in a heatproof bowl over a pan of barely simmering water. Set aside to cool slightly.

In another bowl, sift together the flour and baking powder, then stir in the salt and set aside. In a separate bowl, whisk together the eggs, sugar and vanilla until frothy, then whisk in the melted butter. Fold in the dry ingredients until just mixed, then fold in the chocolate pieces. Pour into your prepared baking tin.

Bake in the middle of the oven for about 35 mins. A skewer inserted should come out ever so slightly gooey. Leave to cool completely in the baking tin, then cut into smallish squares. These are rich!

Peanut butter cookies taste even better when sandwiched with a peanut butter cream. These cookies have a little crunch to them which is a nice contrast in texture to the lighter-than-air filling.

PEANUT BUTTER SANDWICH COOKIE

Filling suggestion: Peanut Butter Cream (Recipe on page 146)

Makes 24

180g plain flour
¾ tsp bicarbonate of soda
A pinch of salt
225g unsalted butter, softened
200g light brown sugar
1 large egg
1 large egg yolk
200g crunchy peanut butter
1 tsp pure vanilla extract
Small packet of roasted salted peanuts

Preheat the oven to 180°C/gas 4. Line 2 trays with baking paper.

In a bowl, sift together the flour and bicarbonate of soda. Stir in the salt and set aside.

In a separate bowl, cream together the softened butter and the sugar until light and fluffy, using an electric hand whisk or a freestanding mixer fitted with the flat beater. Add the egg and the egg yolk and mix well. Add the peanut butter and vanilla to the butter mixture and mix well. Slowly add the dry ingredients, mixing until just incorporated. Chill for about 1 hour.

Drop 48 small scoops of batter, about 5cm apart, onto the prepared trays. Press half a peanut (flat-side up) into each ball of dough. Bake in the middle of the oven for 15–18 mins or until set and slightly golden.

Remove from the oven to a wire rack and cool completely.

To assemble:
Spread a generous scoop of Peanut Butter Cream (page 146) on the flat side of a cooled peanut butter cookie. Top with another cookie, and serve.

PEANUT BUTTER CREAM

Makes enough to fill 24 peanut butter sandwich cookies

225g unsalted butter, softened
250g crunchy peanut butter
300g icing sugar
¼ tsp pure vanilla extract

In a bowl, cream the softened butter, peanut butter and sugar together until light and fluffy, using an electric hand whisk or a freestanding mixer fitted with the flat beater. Whip until light and fluffy and pale in colour. Add the vanilla and whip to mix.

Chill until ready to use. Will keep in a sealed container in the fridge for 1 week. (You can also use this peanut butter cream filling in a chocolate whoopie pie, for a delicious, super-rich snack.)

This is a simple version of the chocolate macaroons that I learned to make at Pierre Hermé's pastry school in Paris. Pierre is a genius and his pastries are the best in the world.

CHOCOLATE MACAROONS

Filling suggestion: Chocolate-Caramel Ganache (Recipe on page 150)

Makes 20 macaroon sandwiches

100g icing sugar, plus an extra 2 tbsp
50g unsweetened cocoa powder
100g ground almonds
2 large egg whites

Preheat the oven to 200°C/gas 6. Line 2 trays with baking paper.

In the bowl of a food processor, blend the 100g icing sugar with the cocoa powder and ground almonds for about 3 mins. Sift into a large bowl and set aside.

In a separate bowl, whisk the egg whites with the 2 tbsp icing sugar until billowy peaks form and the mixture is smooth and glossy, but not dry. Fold half of the dry ingredients into the egg whites and then fold in the remainder. Transfer the mixture to a piping bag fitted with a 1cm tip.

Create a template by tracing 20 small circles about 5cm apart on a sheet of paper and placing it underneath the baking paper on one of the prepared baking trays (so that you can use the template again). Pipe 20 small rounds of batter onto the baking paper on the first tray, then remove the template, place it under the baking paper on the next tray, and repeat. Remember to remove the template.

Tap the trays on your work surface to release any air in the macaroons. Leave to dry out for 20 mins. Place in the 200°C/gas 6 oven and immediately turn the oven down to 180°C/gas 4. Bake for 2 mins, then reduce the oven temperature to 160°C/gas 3 and bake for 2 mins more. Reduce the oven temperature to 140°C/gas 1 and bake for a further 4 mins. (Total baking time is 8 mins.)

Remove from the oven to a wire rack and cool completely.

To assemble:
Spread a generous scoop of Chocolate-Caramel Ganache (page 150) on the flat surface of a cooled macaroon. Top with another macaroon, and serve.

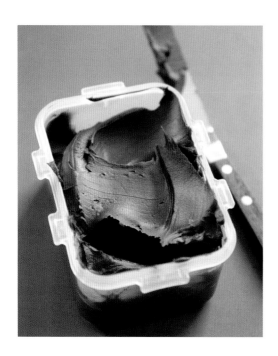

CHOCOLATE-CARAMEL GANACHE

Makes enough to fill about 20 macaroons

150g dark chocolate, finely chopped
2 tbsp cold water
100g caster sugar
120g double cream
25g unsalted butter
Pinch of sea salt

Place the chocolate in a large, heatproof bowl and set aside.

Put the water in a heavy-bottomed saucepan. Add the caster sugar and heat gently to dissolve, swirling the contents around without stirring. Once the sugar has dissolved, turn the heat up to high and bring to the boil. Cook until the caramel is dark. Whisk in the cream, taking care not to splash. Add the butter and salt and whisk until smooth.

Pour the caramel over the chopped chocolate and whisk gently until smooth and melted. Allow to set at room temperature for 2 hours until it is of a spreadable consistency. Will keep in a sealed container in the fridge for 1 week.

Many of you will already have all the equipment and tools that you need for the job of making whoopie pies: weighing scales, a large mixing bowl or two, measuring spoons, a good whisk, baking trays.

TECHNIQUES & EQUIPMENT

If you are interested in getting a little more serious about your baking and want to achieve foolproof results, then I highly recommend a freestanding mixer such as a KitchenAid or Kenwood mixer. The flat beater paddle attachment will cream the butter and sugar until perfectly light and fluffy, and the whisk will give you billowy white meringues and Swiss buttercream icings.

A tool that I find indispensable in the Violet kitchen for making the whoopie pie cakes is the ice cream scoop. The ones with quick-release handles will give the perfect shape to your whoopies and they come in many different sizes. For most of the whoopie pie recipes here, I suggest a 4cm-diameter ice cream scoop with trigger for large whoopies and a small scoop for mini whoopies. They are available from good cookshops and online. Or you can simply use a tablespoon or teaspoon to scoop up the mixture and a second one to scrape it onto your prepared baking trays.

For filling whoopie pies, I use either a piping bag with a large round tip, or a couple of spoons. I scoop up the filling with one spoon and then scrape it off onto the flat side of one whoopie with the other. This works very well but if you prefer a more perfect and refined whoopie, then use a piping bag and pipe perfect blobs onto half of your upturned whoopies and then sandwich them together, pressing until the filling comes to the edge.

For some of these recipes, you may need to bake the whoopie cakes in two batches, depending on the size of your oven and baking trays. Unless otherwise specified, once the cakes come out of the oven transfer them to a wire rack, still on their baking trays, and leave to cool before assembling the pies. Once assembled, most whoopie pies would keep overnight in an airtight container – if you can resist tempation that long.

I have recommended the particular fillings, toppings and sauces that are ideal flavour combinations for each whoopie. But you can get creative and mix and match the recipes any way you like.

INDEX

ACKNOWLEDGEMENTS

Huge thanks to the Violet Girls: Ana, Shailee, Peta, Jane and Echo for everything they do every day at Violet. And a very special thank you to Adriana (Dri) Nascimento for giving so much time and dedication, and for making all of us laugh all the time. And thank you to the men of Violet: Michel, Dino, and Mitesh for driving us to work, letting us work long hours and for sampling lots of cakes.

I am so grateful to my neighbours Henry, Jemima, George and Johnny Dimbleby and Roland, Susan, and Nellie Mae Chambers for eating ridiculous amounts of whoopie pies and for being Violet's best customers. Thanks to Isla and Cameron too, for stamping bags.

Thank you also to my agent Antony Topping for photographing me with Talulla's school bear; to my editor Rowan Yapp for trust and belief and for giving me the freedom to make this book look the way I wanted; to Jan Bowmer and Elisabeth Ptak for their fantastic edits; to Friederike Huber and Anna Crone for beautiful design and of course a big thank you to Colin "Big C" Campbell for his inspired photographs and for his unparalleled work ethic.

Finally, thanks to Damian, for everything.

ABOUT THE AUTHOR

Claire Ptak is an American pastry chef who moved to London in 2005 after working at Chez Panisse restaurant in Berkeley, California. She owns Violet, a baking company in East London. Her popular stall in Broadway Market is best known for its American-style cupcakes with seasonal buttercream frostings. She recently opened a café and cake shop nearby, where whoopie pies have become a much-loved fixture.

www.violetcakes.com